SPORTS TO THE EXTREME

EXTREME Air Sports

BY ERIN K BUTLER

raintree
a Capstone company — publishers for children

Raintree is an imprint of Capstone Global Library Limited, a company incorporated in England and Wales having its registered office at 264 Banbury Road, Oxford, OX2 7DY – Registered company number: 6695582

www.raintree.co.uk
myorders@raintree.co.uk

Edited by Nikki Ramsay
Designed by Sara Radka
Production by Laura Manthe

ISBN 978-1-4747-4792-9 (library binding)
22 21 20 19 18 17
10 9 8 7 6 5 4 3 2 1

British Library Cataloguing in Publication Data
A full catalogue record for this book is available from the British Library.

Acknowledgements
iStockphoto: cover, 1; Newscom: EPA/AZHAR RAHIM, 5; Shutterstock: 6 (top), 6 (bottom), 9, 10, 13, 21; Newscom: ZUMAPRESS/Jay Nemeth, 11; Getty Images: Moment Open, 14; Getty Images: iStockphoto, 15; Getty Images: Flickr RF, 17; Getty Images: Aurora Open, 19; Shutterstock: Alexandra Lande, 22; Shutterstock: Sergei Bachlakov, 25; Newscom: ZUMAPRESS/Nikos Pilos, 26; Getty Images: David Cannon/Laureus, 27; Shutterstock: LeoBrogioni, 27; Newscom: Novespace/Sipa USA, 29

Graphic elements by Book Buddy Media.

The publisher does not endorse products whose logos may appear on objects in images in this book.

Every effort has been made to contact copyright holders of material reproduced in this book. Any omissions will be rectified in subsequent printings if notice is given to the publisher.

All the Internet addresses (URLs) given in this book were valid at the time of going to press. However, due to the dynamic nature of the Internet, some addresses may have changed, or sites may have changed or ceased to exist since publication. While the author and publisher regret any inconvenience this may cause readers, no responsibility for any such changes can be accepted by either the author or the publisher.

Contents

Extreme air sports

The sun beats down on your face as you feel the wind whipping through your hair. The ground feels kilometres away, and your heart is pumping faster than you thought possible. You are excited, but you also know there is danger. And that danger is thrilling. This is the world of extreme air sports.

Extreme air sports are not your average sporting events. They are high-speed, high-risk sports performed in the air. The people who perform them thrive on seeking thrills and getting their adrenaline pumping by defying gravity.

The world of extreme air sports is a highly specialized one. Most extreme air sports require equipment, such as harnesses, specially designed ropes, suits, gliders or even planes. With so many diverse and exciting air sports to choose from, there is a lot of room for creativity.

EXTREME FACT!

Extreme sports can be dangerous. Between 2000 and 2011, they led to more than 4 million injuries. Injuries ranged from strains and sprains to broken bones, concussions and traumatic brain injuries.

BASE jumpers leap from tall structures all around the world, such as the Kuala Lumpur Tower in Malaysia.

Bungee jumpers need to make sure their ropes are the right length so they will not hit the ground.

THE BIGGEST JUMP

The Royal Gorge Bridge in Cañon City, Colorado, USA, is the highest place to bungee jump. This suspension bridge offers a jump of 321 metres (1,053 feet). However, the park has recently stopped allowing jumpers.

Bungee jumping

Today bungee jumping has become a popular and well-known activity. Many people – not just sportspeople – go bungee jumping for fun. It involves jumping from a high place, with an elastic cord attached to your body or ankles. The cord stops you just before you reach the ground. Different types of jumps can be performed to vary the experience of the fall. The bravest jumpers leap at night, blind to what may be in front of – or below – them.

Bungee jumping was first practised on Pentecost Island, in the South Pacific. People would jump from tall heights with vines wrapped round their ankles. Later, thrill-seeking adventurers replaced the vines with rubber elastic cords.

Over the years, bungee jumping has evolved into the extreme sport we know today. And extreme athletes are always looking for ways to raise the stakes. For example, they may perform jumps without an extra safety harness or jump head first rather than feet first or backwards.

EXTREME FACT!

South African jumper Mohr Keet holds the record for being the world's oldest bungee jumper. He performed a jump at the age of 96.

CHAPTER 2

Skydiving

When people think of extreme sports, skydiving is often one of the first things that come to mind. Nothing sounds more outrageous than jumping out of a plane with only a parachute to guide you to safety! Some people do this as a one-time activity just for fun. Others spend years practising their craft to become truly extreme skydivers.

Modern parachuting began in France in the late 1700s. In 1797 a man called André-Jacques Garnerin began jumping from hot air balloons and landing with a parachute. Later, people started to use aeroplanes instead. As plane technology improved, the height a skydiver could jump from went up too. Today extreme skydivers jump from planes flying at **altitudes** as high as 4,600 m (15,000 feet).

Competitive skydiving dates back to the 1930s. The first World Parachuting Championships took place in 1951, in what was then Yugoslavia. Today skydivers can compete in a number of different ways. Some try to reach the highest speeds possible. Others try to land on small targets. In some competitions, skydivers make formations in a group or perform special acrobatic moves while falling.

altitude – how high a place is above sea level

New skydivers train by leaping out of planes with experienced jumpers.

Sometimes a group of skydivers will jump in formation. Holding each others' hands and feet, divers can make interesting shapes as they fall.

There's more to skydiving than just jumping. The standard falling position is belly-to-earth. In this position, the skydiver jumps with his or her stomach facing the ground. Once a skydiver jumps out of the plane, he or she is in freefall until the parachute is deployed. Freefall can last from 40 to 85 seconds. Extreme skydivers can reach high falling speeds. The average speed is between 177 and 209 km (110 and 130 miles) per hour. World records for skydiving speeds in competitions are even higher – more than 595 km (370 miles) per hour!

A skydiver needs a lot of equipment to stay safe. The most important piece of equipment is the parachute, also called the main canopy. The parachute and the reserve parachute are held in a backpack called the container. A skydiver wears the container with shoulder and leg straps attached.

When the skydiver is ready to deploy the parachute, he or she throws a small parachute, called the pilot chute. The pilot chute unfolds. As it catches the air, it pulls the main canopy out of the container and allows the diver to float gently to the ground.

SUPER SPEED

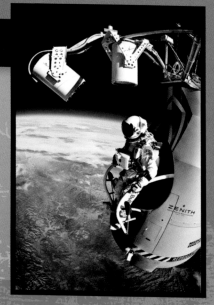

In 2012 Felix Baumgartner set the record for the world's highest skydive. He jumped from 39,014 m (128,000 feet), reaching speeds of nearly 1,175 km (730 miles) per hour. It took him 4 minutes, 22 seconds to reach Earth's surface.

Freeflying

Over the years, many different types of skydiving have been invented. One of the most extreme and popular types is freeflying, which began in the 1990s. In freeflying, skydivers use traditional skydiving positions, but they also extend into a vertical position while in freefall. This means that they fall faster on average than a skydiver. And unlike skydiving, which can be done by almost anyone with assistance, freeflying takes years of training to master.

In freeflying, skydivers can use different jump orientations to fall either head first or feet first. Some freeflying skydivers start out in the belly-to-earth position, known as box position. Others use different positions, such as back flying, head-up flying, head-down flying, and side flying. Then, the skydiver extends his or her legs to fall straight down in a vertical position.

A skydiver must have lots of practice to begin freeflying. When freeflying, skydivers can reach an average speed of more than 257 km (160 miles) per hour. These high speeds make this type of skydiving even more dangerous.

EXTREME FACT!

The most advanced freeflying positions, such as head-down and sit flying, can allow a jumper to fall more than 322 km (200 miles) per hour.

To start freeflying, a person must first master standard skydiving.

13

BASE jumping

For some adrenaline junkies, skydiving was not extreme enough. They decided to up the stakes by inventing BASE jumping. Instead of leaping from a plane, jumps are made from stationary objects – buildings, antenna towers, spans (also known as bridges) and earth. Like skydiving, parachutes are used. But BASE jump locations are much closer to the ground. This means there is not much time to deploy a parachute.

Buildings, antenna towers and spans are man-made, and it can be difficult to gain access to them for jumping. The last type, earth, includes natural formations, such as cliffs and mountainsides.

In many places, BASE jumping is illegal. It is very dangerous. Since the surfaces are so close to the ground – generally between 305 to 610 m (1,000 to 2,000 feet) high – there is no room for error in deploying the parachute. Jumpers also risk hitting the objects from which they jump.

TAKE A NUMBER

When a BASE jumper has jumped off one of each type of object, he or she can apply for a number from the US BASE Association. The number tells them how many people have completed the challenge before them.

Extreme athletes enjoy the thrill of a crazy stunt, such as BASE jumping off a cliff over a body of water, because it is so dangerous.

Wingsuit flying

For centuries humans have been trying to figure out how to fly like birds. While this is still something outside our reach, extreme athletes have come very close with wingsuit flying. This highly specialized form of skydiving involves a unique suit. This suit allows a flyer to soar over the earth before deploying a parachute and landing.

The secret to flying is the wingsuit itself. Wingsuits work because of the physics of flying. They are designed to increase the surface area of the flyer. Webbing between the legs and under each arm create "wings". The webbing is made of strong fabric and has special **air cells** that inflate when they catch the air.

When a flyer wears a wingsuit, he or she is able to **descend** at a slower rate and stay in freefall longer. He or she can also travel much greater distances. Unlike skydivers, who fall more vertically, wingsuit flyers travel over a longer horizontal distance as they descend. The longest distance a flyer has glided is 17.7 km (11 miles)!

air cell – a pocket in fabric that can fill up with air, allowing something to take flight

descend – to move from a higher place to a lower place

During long wingsuit flights, flyers can get a beautiful view of the earth below.

Extreme zip-lining

Lots of skill and practice is required for many extreme sports. But there are a few activities in which anyone in good physical shape can participate. One of these sports is extreme zip-lining.

Zip-line tracks stretch over valleys and canyons. Metal cables and pulleys allow a person wearing a harness to speed from the top of the track to the bottom. Zip-liners can reach speeds up to 161 km (100 miles) per hour.

Like many other extreme sports, zip-lining began as a practical way to travel. Even in ancient times, people used zip lines as a way to cross difficult **terrain** or reach **remote** areas.

For extreme zip-liners, two main factors are speed and distance. Zip-liners get a thrill from speeding as fast as possible along the cables. They can reach higher speeds when tracks are longer. The longest zip line in the world, Puerto Rico's "The Monster", is nearly 2.4 km (1.5 miles) long.

terrain – the surface of the land
remote – far away, isolated or distant

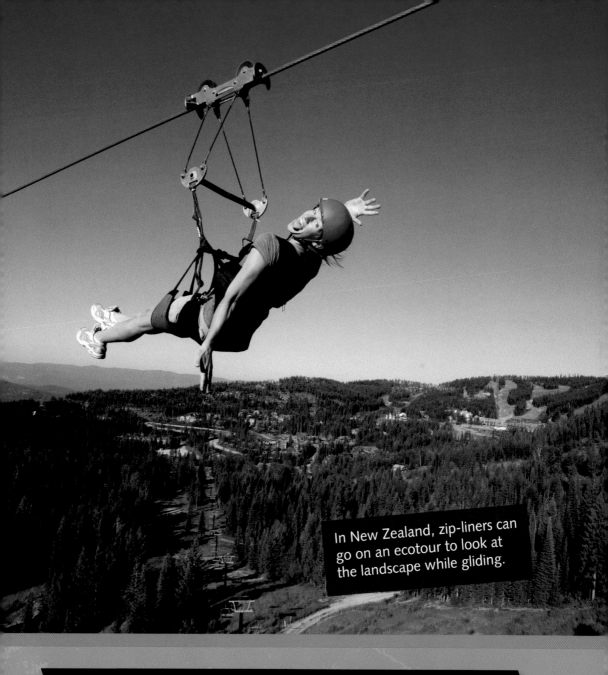

In New Zealand, zip-liners can go on an ecotour to look at the landscape while gliding.

AROUND THE WORLD

Some of the world's most extreme zip-lines are found in Arenal Volcano National Park in Costa Rica, Sun City in South Africa, and Flight of the Gibbon in Thailand.

CHAPTER 6

Gliding

Many people want to know what it feels like to fly without the help of an aeroplane. Gliding is one way to do that. A non-powered aircraft gives them the lift to leave the ground. The best type of non-powered aircraft to use is a **sailplane**.

The most popular gliding sports are general gliding, paragliding, and hang-gliding. When gliding competitively, gliders compete for distance, speed, and height gained.

Paragliding

When paragliding, the glider is strapped into a harness. The harness is attached to a rectangular parachute with cords called lines. To begin, the glider inflates the air cells on the parachute. Then he or she runs down a slope until there is enough speed to launch into flight. He or she flies at a speed of about 19 km (12 miles) per hour.

Parachutes are made out of strong, tear-proof **synthetic** fabric with air pockets that fill with wind. The parachute does not have a **rigid** frame. It can be steered by the paraglider's body position and use of the lines.

Extreme paragliders can fly long distances. Many can glide more than 161 km (100 miles) during a single flight. In competitions, paragliders show off their skills by flying to points far away. Average paragliding speeds are 27 to 45 km (17 to 28 miles) per hour.

Paragliding can give flyers a bird's-eye view of beautiful landscapes and mountains.

sailplane – a light, unpowered aircraft that can be lifted up by the air

synthetic – something that is made by people rather than found in nature

rigid – inflexible; not easy to bend

hang-glider

parachute

The world's best hang-gliders enter competitions such as the Grininko Hang Gliding Competition in Crimea, Ukraine.

Hang-gliding

Hang-gliding is very similar to paragliding, but there are some big differences. The most important difference is the aircraft itself. Hang-gliders have rigid frames made of hard metal. They are covered with lightweight fabric, such as nylon or Dacron. Because of this structure, the gliders cannot control their flight the same way that paragliders do. Someone who is hang gliding must shift his or her body weight to steer the aircraft.

Early hang-gliders were made of heavy materials and were difficult to steer. A major improvement in steering came when swing seats were developed. Today, even after much improvement, gliders are still looking for ways to improve the aircraft. Thanks to new designs, modern hang-gliders can have a **glide ratio** of more than 20 to 1. This means that for every 6 m (20 feet) forwards a hang-glider sails, the aircraft descends 0.3 m (1 foot). This is a great improvement from the first glide ratios, which were about 3 to 1!

Hang-gliders can travel faster than paragliders, up to about 100 km (62 miles) per hour. They can also travel long distances. The best hang gliders have traveled more than 483 km (300 miles).

glide ratio – the ratio of how far an object glides horizontally to how far it drops vertically

Highlining

The extreme sport of highlining comes from a much tamer activity known as slacklining. In slacklining, a person attaches a thin strip of nylon webbing between two fixed points, often the bases of tree trunks. Then, starting at one end, the slackliner walks to the other end of the line.

Highlining raises the stakes. The line is dozens – or even hundreds – of metres off the ground. Any misstep could mean severe injury or death.

One thing that makes highlining so difficult is the line itself. The nylon material is not sturdy like a balance beam. Because it is flexible, it bends with the highliner's weight. The line is also very thin, usually about 2.5 centimetres (1 inch) thick. It is essential that the highliner attaches the line properly to anchors on each end so that the line does not fall. The line must be anchored to a sturdy object that can support the highliner's weight.

Balance is the other challenge highliners face. They do not use anything to help them keep their balance while crossing the line. Instead, highliners rely on stretching out their arms and having a good sense of their own body. Balancing on a highline can be difficult to master.

EXTREME FACT!

Highliners come together every year for the Urban Highline Festival in Poland.

It is important to anchor the line securely on objects that can support the weight of a person.

Highlining allows people to see amazing parts of the world from a new perspective – and with an added adrenaline rush. People have set up highlines all over the world. Deserts, mountains, water and canyons all offer different highline experiences. Some of the most famous places for highlining include eastern France; Kjerag Lysefjorden, Norway; and locations in the USA including Utah and Yosemete Falls, California.

No matter how extreme a sport, competitors are always looking for ways to take things to the next level. They want to cross longer lines at taller heights. Danny Menšík and Nathan Paulin hold the record for crossing the world's longest highline. This highline is located in Aiglun, France, and is a whopping 1,020 m (3,347 feet) long!

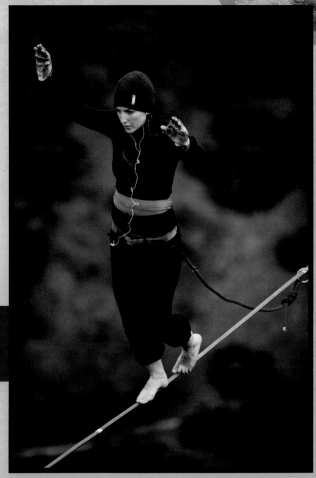

Professional highliner Faith Dickey has paved the way for women in this extreme sport.

Every year there are slackline festivals held around the world in many beautiful locations. In 2017 a festival was held in Barão de Cocais, Brazil.

DEAN POTTER

One of the most famous faces in extreme sports was Dean Potter. Potter was a climber, highliner, BASE jumper and wingsuit flyer. He was not only skilled, but also creative. Sometimes, he borrowed from different extreme sports to create one thrilling adventure. For example, he combined wingsuit flying and BASE jumping. Potter was well known in the highlining world because of his daring adventures without safety nets. Potter died in a BASE jumping accident in 2015 after the parachute of his wingsuit didn't deploy.

Zero-G flight experience

In extreme air sports, the sky is the limit. But extreme adventurers have set their sights even higher – outer space! To get a feel for weightlessness without leaving Earth, they can join a Zero-G flight experience.

The Zero-G flight experience takes place on a specially designed aeroplane. Once the plane flies to a height of 7,315 m (24,000 feet), the pilot begins a series of manoeuvres called **parabolas**. During each parabola, passengers in the plane experience 20 to 30 seconds of weightlessness. In total, a Zero-G flight experience plane will fly 15 parabolas per session.

There is little gravity in space, and a Zero-G flight experience feels a lot like space travel. While weightless, people can float, flip and soar in ways that are not possible in any other place on Earth. This is truly the new frontier for extreme air sports.

The Zero-G flight experience is currently used for recreation. Participants do not need to be extreme athletes. Anyone in good health can participate, and children as young as 8 years old have done Zero-G. After taking a brief class, they are ready to be weightless.

There is plenty of room for advancement in the future of Zero-G and other extreme sports. Without creativity, bravery and a little technology, air sports wouldn't be the extreme activities we know today.

parabola – a curve that follows the shape of an object that is thrown into the air and falls down

Before going up into the air, participants complete a course to learn all about Zero-G.

EXTREME FACT!

During a Zero-G flight experience, a person undergoes a total of about eight minutes of weightlessness.

Glossary

air cell a pocket in fabric that can fill up with air, allowing something to take flight

altitude how high a place is above sea level

descend to move from a higher place to a lower place

glide ratio the ratio of how far an object glides horizontally to how far it drops vertically

parabola a curve that follows the shape of an object that is thrown into the air and falls down

remote far away, isolated, or distant

rigid inflexible; not easy to bend

sailplane a light, unpowered aircraft that can glide through the air

synthetic something that is made by people rather than found in nature

terrain the surface of the land

Find out more

Air Sports (Extreme Sport), Ellen Labreque (Raintree, 2011)

Extreme Skydiving (Nailed It!), Virginia Loh-Hagan (Cherry Lake Publishing, 2016)

Extreme Skysurfing (Sports on the Edge!), Tamra B Orr (Marshall Cavendish, 2014)

Extreme Sports (The Wimp's Guide), Tracey Turner (Franklin Watts, 2013)

Websites

http://www.sciencekids.co.nz/sciencefacts/sports/extremesports.html

http://www.telegraph.co.uk/news/worldnews/australiaandthepacific/newzealand/3448598/Bungee-jumping-20-facts.html

http://pbskids.org/dragonflytv/show/paragliding.html

http://sciencelearn.org.nz/Contexts/Flight/Looking-Closer/Hang-gliders

Index